IN THE PALMS OF ANGELS

POETRY BY

TERRI KIRBY ERICKSON

Press 53
Winston-Salem

Press 53
PO Box 30314
Winston-Salem, NC 27130

First Edition

Cover design by Kevin Morgan Watson

Cover art, "Frances," Copyright © 2011 by Stephen White

Cover art photograph by Dan Rossi

Chapter art photographs by Leonard Erickson

Author cover photograph by Superieur Photographics

Printed on acid-free paper

ISBN 978-1-935708-27-8

for Leonard

ACKNOWLEDGMENTS

Many thanks to the editors of the following publications where these poems (and in a few cases, earlier versions of these poems), first appeared:

A Prairie Journal: "Sunflowers"
Basilica Review: "Rosary"
Bay Leaves: "Topsail Island"
Between the Lines Cape Fear River Foundation Chapbook (2009 and 2010): "Granny Smith Apple," "Road Crew," "Sam White," "Boogie-Woogie"
Broad River Review: "Incident on the Train," "Waves"
Dead Mule: "Denise and Merle," "Crystal Clear"
Eclectica: "Things We Should Learn in First Grade," "Miller Street"
Flutter: "Back Porch Blues"
Forsyth Woman: "Homecoming" (published as, "Edwin")
Foundling Review: "Farmers' Market"
Hektoen International, A Journal of Medical Humanities: "Breast Cancer Suite"
Imagining Heaven (anthology): "Heaven"
Journal of the American Medical Association: "Cling Peaches," 302(7):722, Copyright © 2009 American Medical Association. All rights reserved.
Long Story Short: "Pompano," "Santo Domingo," "My Daughter's Hair," "The Gardener"
Muse India: "Woman in Delhi"
Nibble: "Sponge Bath"
North Carolina Literary Review: "Making the Biscuits"

Oak Bend Review: "Young Girl at Walgreen's"
Old Mountain Press Anthologies: *The Outer Side of Life*,
    "Mrs. Listner's Chickens"; *Just Between Us*: "Uncle
    John's '55 Fairlane"; *Mountain High*: "Appalachia";
    Traveling Time: "Riding Gun's Bicycle to Lake Mälaren"
Pinesong: "At the Drive-In"
Port City Poets: "From the Garden"
Prairie Wolf Press: "Night Train"
Scythe: "Girl in a Green Dress," "Darla's Daughter," "To
    My Brother Who Died a Virgin"
Seeding the Snow: "Butterfly Bush"
Smoking Poet: "At the Nursing Home"
Still Crazy: "At the Pediatrician's Office"
The Sound of Poets Cooking: (Anthology, Jacar Press),
    "Granny Smith Apple"
Time of Singing: "Love"
Toasted Cheese: "Downpour"
Tryst: "Depression"
Shoal: "Shrimp Boat Captain"
Wild Goose Poetry Review: "Uncle Jack"

Award-Winning Poems:
"Wedding Days," First Place in the "Love" Category of
    The Writers' Ink Guild Fields of Earth poetry contest,
    2010
"Topsail Island," Second Place, Poetry Council of North
    Carolina, James Larkin Pearson Contest for Free
    Verse, 2009
"At the Drive-In," Third Place, North Carolina Poetry
    Society Mary Ruffin Poole American Heritage Award,
    2010
"Shrimp Boat Captain," First Place, Poetry, Carteret
    Writers 19th Annual Writing Contest

CONTENTS

Introduction
by Ron Powers

You might say that as a poet, Terri Kirby Erickson is fortunate to live in North Carolina.

Truer to say that as a poet, Terri Erickson *is* North Carolina.

She is far from the only artist who can claim this exalted merging of identities, of course. Thomas Wolfe's "Old Catawba" endures as one of the great fertile seedbeds of the American voice. The metaphor is apt. Words seem to rise up from the state's very earth, nourished by the compost of memory and music and eulogy and superstition and tale and prayer. The words rise up, and take possession of those who know how to listen. Who, in turn, teach the rest of us how to listen. Terri Kirby Erickson is among the living best of these knowers and teachers.

The compost upon which she draws has been thickening through four centuries. It formed the topsoil from which flourished the banjo picking and the "Jack" tales up in the northwestern Great Smokies—transplants from Scotland. It spilled into the rolling hills of Carrboro in Orange County, where the young housemaid "Libba" Cotten watched freight trains rolling past, and then sang them into folk myth while playing her guitar left-handed and upside-down.

It has infused the stories still told by Cherokee bards along an infamous arc in the southwest corner, where ski slopes otherwise obscure the Trail of Tears. It accumulates in the rural western hills around Canton, where a fantasy-addled young Tar Heel named Fred Chappell rose from farmhand to great distinction as a poet, novelist and scholar. It found a welcome even around the now-defunct textile mills in Asheboro, where Barbara Presnell grew up hearing her kinfolk talk their plain talk about doing piecework, and heard the poetry in that talk, and wrote it down to keep it pulsing forever.

Up in Macon (pop. 115) on the Virginia border, the great Reynolds Price scooped up that compost of voices from the played out cotton and tobacco fields and slathered it richly over his novels and stories. "He made this small corner of North Carolina the sovereign territory of his own imagination," is the way his fellow Tar Heel Alan Garganus (Rocky Mount) eulogized him.

In Terri Kirby Erickson's case, that divine compost seems no farther beyond her reach than the beds of hyacinths and tulips that grow on her lawn just beyond her front porch in Lewisville, or the tomato patches on the side. Terri Erickson is an inspired conduit of North Carolina voices, past and present, and they keep up a lively disputatious chatter throughout her pages:

> The boss kept hinting that she ought to retire, but Clovis knew the score. He was itching to hire one of them girls from up at the community college
>
> who kept coming around filling out applications, which Clovis chucked in the garbage can when nobody
>
> was looking. *Buzzards*, she muttered under her breath. The nerve of them girls, circling her job while she was still in it. . .

Ms. Erickson is a poet of continuity. As her compatriots in the region have long done, she seamlessly blends the vernacular voices of the characters in her poems with her own attentive yet restrained vernacular diction, collapsing the distances between herself and her people, the past and the present, daily reality and timeless myth. Not to mention pathos and humor. Here is an old woman responding, as tears stream down her face, to a boy who has asked how come she eats onions all day.

". . . Could be, I like the taste of onions,"
she said, leaning in close. "I bet you cry on a dime,
don't you, boy?" Too scared to lie, he nodded.
"Next time, thank the Lord Jesus for them tears.
Some people can't cry—even when the pain's
so bad, they is on their knees. If I didn't eat onions,"
she said, pulling a choice Vidalia from the bucket,
"I'd drown in misery that won't come out."

The Onion Eater shares a universe of ordinary saints and sinners who are at once specific to their region and—well—universal: women in cancer wards, women in nursing homes who wear pastel housecoats with front pockets and thin white socks, women in grocery store parking lots "sharing sadness like a loaf of warm bread." You will find folks like Brother Bob Braithwaite, on his knees in his church office moaning, *Steeped in a vat of sin is what I am,*" while Louise Hickman, his administrative assistant, mutters, "probably for some minor offense like jaywalking or saying *gosh darn.*" You will encounter confused young girls in bus stations daring to believe they "have what it takes to become/a famous movie star or even a movie star's girlfriend,/which might be even better." And you are likely to run into the wrongo Billy Cisco, who clawed his way out of his mother's womb, played mean pranks in school and ended up trying to rob the First Citizen's Bank with a BB gun, while wearing a stolen chicken suit formerly owned by his ex-wife's brother. Don't worry; he was caught and locked up. His crossed eyes gave him away.

The playful comic strain is of course impossible to miss in these little portraits, but Southern-gothic riffing is far from Ms. Erickson's main concern. (You may have noticed that I do not refer to her, in the oh-so-fashionable manner, as "Erickson." This is because I am flat scared that if I did, her Grandmother would jump out of the pages and come at me with her pompano-slicing knife for my vulgarity toward a Lady).

What is she after, then?

To some extent (as with all good artists), that is for Terri Erickson to know and you to find out. Or to collaborate with her in finding out. Which can be a most congenial process, as her loyal readers understand. Certainly she will never be mistaken for one of those fancy "workshop" poets, or MFA poets, or gender-identity poets or what-have-you, always throwing hermeneutical challenges or exegesistic conundrums in your way. She's an affable soul, but try laying a hand on one of her lines of imagery and suggesting that it might be just a tad more, you know, *abstruse* or something, and you're likely to be soaking your knuckles in ice-water for a spell. Her work often shows a quality, quietly defiant and deceptive, of plainsong, of utter unconcealment, that might strike an academic eye as artless. In Ms. Erickson's hands, this quality is itself an art: a brave refusal to be diverted by received mannerism; an unrelenting resolve to burn through into what the Tennessean James Agee called "The cruel radiance of what is."

I said up above that Ms. Erickson is a poet of continuity, but that is not the whole story. Her continuity is always dogged at varying distances by separation, by loss, by the danger of meaning giving way to emptiness. One of them girls from the community college is probably going to get Clovis's job one of these days. In some of her poems the worst has already happened. "The old ways are dying," announces the first line of "Appalachia." A brother dies still a virgin: "All you ever knew of naked women was that wet,/wadded-up magazine you and your buddies/ found in a drainpipe."

There is no store-bought redemption pasted to the ends of these poems, but neither will you find hopelessness, self-pity, a turning away from the world. What you will find at the core of all these poems is the timeless North Carolinian's beneficent but ungilded witnessing; her sturdy acceptance of suffering and death and loss of control . . .

> Well, there is nothing he can
> do to save anyone. He learned that early.
> So he gets in the car and drives
> home to his family, his father's ghost
> clinging to the fender, like rust.

. . .yet, in the very teeth of such inevitabilities, an insistent searching for the holiness that is always to be found (with the poet's help) in the enduring ordinary things: cling peaches, sunlight in a daughter's hair, the half-moon slices of peeled Granny Smith apples, meteors from Perseus, and the gulls in "Topsail Island," wheeling and crying "*Joy, joy, joy,*" as they fly "far out to sea, becoming pinpoints of light."

I

TOPSAIL ISLAND

We knelt near
the shoreline

gathering shells,
pieces of sea glass,

stones. Wind
salted our faces,

sent a kite circling,
filled a red sail.

Curtains danced
in cottage windows;

a flock of gulls
wheeled. *Joy*,

joy, joy, they cried—
flying far out

to sea, becoming
pinpoints of light.

ROAD CREW

Beneath a solitary tree, the men and women
on the road crew eat their lunch. They gather
around this cool patch of earth like cowboys
vying for the best spot beside a campfire—
though it's the land outside their shaded circle
that burns. Nearly knee to knee, they chew
without speaking, their angular faces glistening
with sweat, their clothes streaked with dirt.
You wonder if they dream of traffic cones
and angry, honking drivers—feel, even in sleep,
the scalding heat and red dust rising from the road
as cars crawl by them with their air-conditioners
cranked up, windows rolled tight. Come noon,
however, they trade their hard hats for a soft
canopy of leaves, their hard work for a few minutes
of leisure. Like irises soaking up rainwater,
these blue-jean-clad laborers quench their thirst
and feed their hunger, indifferent to the staring
hordes of people passing by. What matters
is the sheltering shade, the bread in their hands,
and a shared sense of common purpose.

ROSARY

Down by the creek,
we sit on dry
stones,

our shoes and socks
jumbled in a pile.
The sun

warms our toes
and casts its
net of light

from bank to bank,
where willows
trail their

fingers in the water,
and snakes look
like branches

floating by
them. Mosquitoes
lay their eggs

in stagnant pools,
far from leaves
and grasses snagged

by rocks, twisting
in the current.
Tadpoles swim

in tight formation,
wiggling their tails
in tandem,

as salamanders
scuttle by, searching
for places to nap.

Dragonflies hover,
then hurry
away,

their wings
thrumming a one-note
song—while we,

silent as nuns in prayer,
count the beads
of summer.

okay / I like the ending best

UNCLE JACK

He's the wiry one who's never quite in the photograph.
Sometimes it's just a shoulder or maybe the side
of his head, one eye squinting at something off-camera.
I saw a picture of him once, in a sailor suit, smiling—
skin so smooth, it looked like plastic. He seemed
happy then, though perhaps he had a full bottle hidden
under his bunk, and was looking forward to drinking
it later. I was too young at the time to understand
the scowl on Grandma's face when forced to say
his name, or why my aunt tiptoed around her husband,
as if he were asleep. I never actually saw much,
myself, but heard my older cousins say things
like *Jack peed in the kitchen sink again*, which made
no sense to me at all when they had a perfectly nice
bathroom right on the ground floor—and I wondered
how they got away with calling their father *Jack*.
That would never work in our house, but then,
their house was nothing like mine. It was much taller
than the one we lived in, and there were a lot more
children. Doors seemed to slam instead of close—
as if drafts whipped through on a regular basis,
and people yelled *good-bye* like they were never
coming back. And after the divorce, which nobody
talked about, either, Jack moved to Washington, D.C.
and bought a car wash, which seemed ironic because
of the location, but also sad because he spent his days
cleaning other people's stuff when his life was such
a mess. His own children wouldn't give him a cup

of spit if he was dying in the desert, but when he finally did die, they all came to the funeral—keeping their distance from the casket in case he wasn't completely dead.

Good ending

EMPATHY

for Felicia

Close as two women crooning into the same
microphone, they sing their sorrows
to one another in a grocery store parking lot,

keys dangling from their hands, cars waiting
still and silent as good dogs, beside them.

People pass by unnoticed; the sky grows dark.
On and on they stand, rooted to the pavement—

sharing sadness like a loaf of warm bread—
eyes luminous as pearls formed by her friend's

suffering. Perhaps the stars will wish on them
tonight. For even as they part, briefly

touching, their glow is brighter—the ground
lit beneath their feet as they walk away,
each wearing the other woman's shoes.

AT THE NURSING HOME

A man sits by a window in a hallway,
hands limp in his lap,
wheelchair turned away from the sun. A house
this rundown would be condemned—

eyes milky with cataracts, limbs so thin a breeze
could snap them, skin like sheets
of phyllo laid over bone. Yet, he's smiling,
as if he'd drawn the curtains

and inside there are marvels—a Honus Wagner
baseball card, a humidor packed
with hand-rolled cigars—and the woman
he loves holding a wine glass, laughing.

Not very poetic but compassionate observation

Clovis McBride

So what if I'm seventy-five years old?
thought Clovis McBride on a rainy Saturday night
at the diner. *People act*

like I'm near-dead when I can run rings around
ever one of them, she said to herself, eyeing all the bellies

hanging over the bar stools and pushing against tables
like inflatable rafts, getting bigger with every pancake

they shoved into their craws.
The boss kept hinting that she ought to retire, but Clovis
knew the score. He was itching to hire one of them girls
from up at the community college

who kept coming around filling out applications,
which Clovis chucked in the garbage can when nobody

was looking. *Buzzards,* she muttered under her breath.
The nerve of them girls, circling her job while she was still
in it—as if it was just a matter of time before she keeled
over and somebody hauled her old carcass

out the back door. Well, she had news for them.
She'd worked every day of her life since the age of thirteen
and wasn't about to quit now. Just let him try to get rid
of her, why she'd call in favors

from every citizen she ever did a favor for,
which was darn near the whole town, and then he'd see

exactly what the words *empty* and *bankrupt*
really meant. And since the boss also happened

to be her husband of fifty years, he'd have a hard time
getting to sleep every night while she was busy
wringing his scrawny neck.

ORPHAN

A fawn stands in a clearing
by a busy road, spots like bubbles
blown across the brown fur of her back,
legs wobbly. She's like a toddler
swaying above a long flight of stairs,
but there's no mother here to save her—
only a cloud of crows cawing overhead,
the roar of cars racing around a curve,
the silent womb of woods where
she might still turn.

MIZ RUTH

Miz Ruth was our Sunday school teacher
and since she never married, we were her only

children. One of her arms was missing below
the elbow, so she hung her purse on the rosy nub

of flesh there. It looked like such a sensible
arrangement, that women without built-in "hooks"

from which to hang their purses seemed, when
standing next to her, less well designed.

She gave every child two Lorna Doone cookies
and orange juice in a Dixie cup once we were done

with our Bible lesson, then told us stories until our
parents picked us up. Her voice sounded exactly

like honeysuckle would, if plants could talk. And
her best friend, Jesus, was someone we all wanted

to know because Miz Ruth thought so much
of him, she got teary-eyed just saying his name.

DEPRESSION

Her knees nearly buckle with the weight of a new star,
but oh the sweet relief when one of them falls or when
the sun pulls up its rays like rope ladders because light,
even light is too heavy for her to carry now. And look

at her loose grip on the baby's stroller, as if any minute
she might let go. Other mothers' eyes follow their children,
glisten like the wet clay of a newly fashioned Madonna,
but her expression never changes. She sees nothing but

the dull, brown jar where she spends her days alone, its
walls slick and impossible to climb, the lid screwed shut—
feels nothing but cold glass against her back, the tightening
in her chest when she tries to breathe what little air is left.

Santo Domingo

I.

Abuelita follows a respectable distance
from the courting couple. They walk
farther every day, it seems, until her feet
ache inside her tightly laced shoes.
But her granddaughter is a good girl.
Her pace is slow, and she glances over
her shoulder from time to time, making
sure that Abuelita is still there.

II.

Every evening at precisely seven
o'clock, her fiancé walks with her
before dinner. He is very punctual,
one of the many things she likes about him,
including his blue/black hair and clean
dress shirts, the sleeves rolled just so,
revealing his wrists and forearms.
And always, Abuelita is ten steps
behind them. At least she pretends not
to listen, and keeps her thoughts private.

III.
My granddaughter is a good girl,
and this boy will make a fine husband.
He does not grab her hand, nor does he
direct their conversation to himself.
He listens respectfully when she speaks,
matches his footsteps to hers.

IV.
My grandmother is very old, so old
her skin is wrinkled and brown as dried
figs, her eyes tucked beneath their lids
like coins under pillows. If Papá
would relent, we could stroll down
the street alone, hold hands like normal
people. Abuelita would be home, napping
in the shade. But no, he says, that path
leads to trouble. It has always been this
way and there is no reason to change.

V.
Soon we will reach the fork in this road,
and perhaps turn back towards home.
Abuelita's mouth waters for fried plantains
and a glass of red wine, rewards
for guarding her granddaughter's virtue.
She knows they meet in secret after dark,
as she had done, and her mother before
her—but appearances must be preserved
until the wedding. Then and only
then, could she rest her poor feet.

BUTTERFLY BUSH

Alive with
wings,

this butterfly
bush

should
lift its

feet,
shake loose

the dirt,
and fly.

CLING PEACHES

ok
very good

I'm sitting by your hospital bed
The morning after we almost lost you—
Feeding you canned peaches with
A plastic spoon. You seldom speak,
With cancer ravaging your fine
Mind like a plague of hungry locusts,
But you seem more yourself today
Than you have in weeks. Your
Gaze is tender as a bruise, and my
Hand trembles, lifting the spoon
To your mouth. Your recent rousing
Performance of *Husband, Dying*,
Has ripped the rose-colored glasses
Right off my face. You aren't going
To get well, after all, despite our
Murmured prayers and midnight
Promises to be good forever, if only.
How like you, though, to hold
A dress rehearsal—eyes shut, your
Leonine head crushing the pillow,
Sheets bunched like drifts of
Snow covering your too-still body.
It became real for me then, your
Death. I wanted to tie you
To the bedrails, stand guard with

A flaming sword, daring anyone,
Anything, to try and take you.
Instead, I feed you cling peaches,
Letting go of you a little more,
My darling, with every bite.

Oh no —
Acceptance to
so hard to
swallow —

II

NIGHT TRAIN

Turning your face to the wall won't stop
the night train roaring past your bedroom
windows, or keep the tattered curtains
from shivering on the sills. Screens will
still lose their footing, tumble into the bushes
below. Your keys will jump and jangle
amidst the loose change and matchbooks
strewn across the dresser. Floorboards
still shake and shimmy to the tune of plates
jiggling in the cabinets down the hall.

And the sound of wheels rumbling down
the tracks reminds you of your teenage
daughter climbing the persimmon tree in
the front yard, waving to all the passengers

as if they could see her fingers fluttering
in the dark. *One day*, you said to yourself,
*she'll buy her own ticket and never come
back*, and that's exactly what she did—your
wife, too. But you've never slept in a room
that doesn't rattle. Your hands cling like
claws to the bed where you were born when
the night train, whistle blowing, rushes toward
God knows where, while you bite your tongue
to keep from crying out, *Wait—Wait for me.*

23

My Daughter's Hair

Sunlight lingers in my daughter's hair,
as if it is captured,

somehow, when she flies across a field,
pulling a kite—or skips though the garden,

gathering flowers. Night and day, it shines,
as if angels run their fingers

through it, when no one's
looking.

DENISE AND MERLE

Denise and Merle work at the *Corner Pharmacy*—
easy jobs compared to what they did before. Merle
sliced lunch meats and hard cheeses, mopped floors
and scoured filthy pans at the *Food Lion* deli,
while Denise waited tables at a truck stop until
bunions, ugly as tree stumps, formed on her feet.
Now all they have to do is help old people find
their favorite talcum powder, locate prescription
bags, neatly labeled, and ring up sales. One evening
close to quitting time, a boy not much older than
Merle's youngest son, pushed through the door.
He seemed nervous and jittery-like, fingering
merchandise all the way down the aisle. Merle
felt a flutter of fear, wishing the pharmacist hadn't
gone home early. It was just the two of them—Merle
at the cash register and Denise, sorting pill bottles.
When he whipped out a gun, Merle wasn't as shocked
as she should have been, but then she kind of saw it
coming. Like somebody in a dream, she pulled money
out of the drawer and stuffed fist-fulls into the smelly
knapsack he thrust under her nose. The boy's narrow
eyes flicked towards Denise, whose jaw dropped
to her chest when he said, *don't move, lady*—
prompting her to scream and run down the hallway,
flinging pill bottles in every direction. When
Merle heard the lock turn in the back room and saw
the robber's panicked expression, she was shocked
beyond belief that her own flesh and blood would

abandon her to the mercy of an armed bandit ready
to snap any minute and riddle the place with bullets.
Thank God he took off instead of shooting her dead,
his rubber-soled shoes squeaking on the polished floor.
When the police came, Denise had the nerve to pretend
she was right beside Merle the whole time, and Merle
kept her mouth shut, too. To this day, they never talk
about the robbery, but Merle stopped leaving her cat
at her sister's when she goes out of town and Denise
won't touch the cash register with a stick, claiming
her arthritis *acts up* when she hits the keys.

Oh my!
Wonderful
story!

To My Brother Who Died a Virgin

All you ever knew of naked women was that wet,
wadded-up magazine you and your buddies
found in a drainpipe. Their heads were thrown

back from their bare breasts like somebody socked
them in the jaw just before he took the pictures.

You never turned into your own driveway
the same time as your wife and kids—tumbled
through the door together and spent the evening

thinking how damn lucky you were, or the whole
night nestled so close to your wife's soft body a slip
of paper wouldn't fit between you. You never

woke up with tears of joy streaming down your face
from a dream that so resembled your real life,

you didn't realize you were sleeping. What you
got instead were the sounds of boys snickering—
sodden photographs of strangers who didn't love you.

Things We Should Learn
in First Grade

Dick, Jane, little Sally and their dog,
Spot, taught me a lot of words, which
I appreciate. But some words are more
important than others and needed stars
beside them to let us know. Even better,
they could have used them in more
meaningful sentences—ones that teach
a lesson you can actually use later in life.
Take for example, the word "run." Run
is a pretty crucial word and needed
rounding out in the meaning department.
How about, "See Jane run because Dick
is messing around with Sally," or, "See
Dick make his third run to the ABC store
in one day," although that might have been
confusing to people just learning the alphabet.
They could even have said, "You can run,
but you can't hide," which would have
applied to Dick, Jane, Sally and Spot,
simultaneously. Instead what we got was,
"See Jane run," without ever knowing
why running was necessary, a lesson best
learned in advance so that when a running
situation comes along, we recognize it
right away rather than three kids, four
rehabs and a nervous breakdown later.

28

GRANNY SMITH APPLE

With shaking hands, he tries to peel
an apple—knife-wielding long gone
from his repertoire of skills.

Soon, he says, I'll forget how
to eat it. So his granddaughter

takes the knife; then, the apple.
Curls of peeling fall to the floor,
where they rest like garden snakes,

basking. Whole orchards never
smelled as good as this, he thinks,

as they savor the half-moon slices—
the old man and his granddaughter,
sharing a Granny Smith apple.

ROSCOE POTEET

Roscoe Poteet was a leader from the start.
He used to lug concrete blocks out by the cornfield
and stand on them, shouting his political philosophy to a gang
of scraggly kids, stray dogs and the occasional

bored teenager, none of whom understood a word
he said, but liked how he said it. They all lived

in the *Happy Camper Trailer Park*, where Roscoe
resided with his aunt and uncle—his parents

having been killed in a car wreck
caused by a moment of inattention, which people seemed
reluctant to talk about so he stopped asking. Eventually

he found out from his second cousin, Curtis,
(who never could keep his mouth shut about anything),

that it was all Roscoe's daddy's fault because he distracted
Roscoe's mama by giving her some neck-sugar
while she was driving the two of them to Morehead City

for a second honeymoon, (her husband having temporarily
lost his license after an unfortunate incident involving

an officer of the law and a pickup truck).
With his mama being so ticklish, particularly in the neck area,
his daddy's poorly-timed smooch made her miss the turnoff

and slam smack into a two-hundred-year-old oak tree
on the outskirts of town. The tree—unlike his parents—
survived the crash, and became a tourist attraction
after Roscoe was elected mayor.

Poor guy.

Sponge Bath

Draped in towels,
my grandmother sits in a hard-backed
chair, a white bowl

of soapy water on the floor.
She lifts her frail arm, then rests it,

gratefully, in her daughter's palm.
Gliding a wet

washcloth, my mother's hand
becomes a cloud, and every bruise, a rain-
drenched flower.

very tender

Miller Street

It seems to him the old house bulges like a can
of beans with botulism—that all the misery contained
within is seeking a way out. Perhaps the glass
in every window will some day shatter, freeing

all the souls trapped there by what happened to them,
who couldn't move on as they say, to the light.
For darkness is a muck that sticks to your shoes,

leaving traces of itself in your sunny new life,
no matter how many times you mop the floors.
Your children will be afraid of you, if only a little,

even if you never raise your voice, even if you make
them blueberry pancakes from scratch every Sunday.
The muck is there, you see, in the brown sludge
of a gaze that oozes from your face like a pus-filled

wound; it pools around the unnatural smile you flash
at your wife, meant to be tender. You can't be
something you don't understand, though he tries;
he tries so hard. But there's a man in his head—

malevolent and taunting—who lived in this house
for years. Even snow melts away from its ancient
shingles with the slightest rise in temperature—
as if loath to brush its white clothes against a thing

that will never be clean. It's for sale again, he sees,
sporting another sign in a long history of signs,
and he pities the people who buy it. His father may
be dead but, oh, he has stained these walls beneath

their fresh coats of paint, with his hate-filled, spittle-
spraying, belt-beating breath—left something
of himself behind like the nicotine-soiled curtains

they'll tell you, come with the house. Well, there
is nothing he can do to save anyone. He learned that
early. So he gets in the car and drives home to his
family, his father's ghost clinging to the fender, like rust.

she mixes 3rd here,
2nd + person
Doesn't work

THE RADIANT

From a point
in Perseus,
meteors
plummet
toward the
earth, tails
blazing.
One flashes
like a bottle
rocket, zooms
along the edge
of the roof,
disappears
from view.
Meteors
seldom hit
the ground,
you tell
me, as if
I've called
you at the
office. *Hold*
my hand,
I say silently.

Hold anything.
But you are
free-falling
and alone.
You burn up
before you
ever reach me.

sounds of regret here,

WOMAN ON THE PHONE ✓

A tired little boy curls on the floor,
on the stair—wherever his mother

stands, talking on the phone. He
clutches a cotton blanket, sucks his

thumb as if his skin is honey. Some
day he'll meet a girl, fall in love.

When she leaves a room, the boy
will feel as if the wind has blown

through it, taking everything. For
now, however, he sees no one but

his mother—as if he is a sunflower,
and she, his only source of light.

The way of a child — yes.

FROM THE GARDEN ✓

for John and Ursula

These are the last of the beans, she said, handing me a sack,
so they won't be as good as the first. We sat a while, in the shade
of twin pecan trees in their backyard, beside the grape arbo
and fig trees, near the summer garden. Her husband laughe

when I confessed I'd never made a pecan pie, and seemed to thin
I should get cracking. He said, *Come by any time—you can have a*
the pecans you can carry. I asked how long they'd been married

and he quickly replied, *She won't tell you*, but it was long enoug
to create this gentle peace between them, no doubt hard wo
If we never fought, it'd be boring, she said with a grin—a gleam
in her eyes that no amount of years could diminish. He grinne

back, and the feeling between them seemed warm and sacre
like a ray of light through a stained glass window. *Be sure*
and add potatoes to your beans she said before I left, her parting

words being, *I wish we'd met you sooner, when the garden*
was full, as if a garden like theirs could ever be empty.

I know about that

Nice

38

Mrs. Listner's Chickens

In Mrs. Listner's chicken coop, a row
of beady-eyed old biddies guarded
their nests, wattles red as blood

on their snow-white necks. "Go on,"
she'd say, "grab an egg," but they
pecked us every time, their beaks sharp

as pencil tips, and we'd draw back
our hands, empty. Then we watched
her gather eggs, quick and easy,

clucking all the while—wattles
wobbling under her chin, hair piled high
on her head like a gray-streaked comb.

HEAVEN

You wake in a sun-drenched room
with knotty pine walls and open windows,

white curtains billowing. The warm,
salt-scented breeze carries

the sound of waves, the laughter of children,
the cry of gulls. Somewhere

inside the house, bacon sizzles in a pan,
coffee drips into a pot—and there are voices,

familiar voices—your grandmother,
your brother, your best friend. It's been

so long since you have seen them.
So you sit up in bed, stretch your strong,

supple limbs. There is no pain,
no stiff shoulders and creaky joints.

There is no weight of sorrow or regret—
only a kind of soaring joy that lifts

and circles inside you like a kite.
And when you move across the floor,

it feels like floating, as if your body is made
of light and air—but solid when

they reach for you, when their arms
open wide and you walk in.

I'm not always interested
in how people
imagine heaven.
This seems okay to me

41

III

Wedding Days

Every day, I marry you again. I wake up,
throw my nightgown in the hamper and take
a shower. I get dressed listening to cardinals
call to one another from tree branch to tree
branch—as if they've known each other for
as long as I've known you. I picture the two
of us sitting in Miss Kattman's Spanish class—
florescent lights bouncing off the smooth planes
of your perfect face. It would pool in every
crease and crevice now, but I like you better this
way. You are more accessible with your rumpled
skin than the *muy guapo* boy you used to be—
the one I couldn't imagine talking to, much less
touching. Now we live in the same house, which
seems like a miracle when I think about it. And
weekdays at 4:58 p.m., you climb the basement
stairs calling my name as if the word itself is a wafer
on your tongue, reach for me as if I am a jeweled
chalice filled with wine. And my body answers
with a kiss, a seal of love that says to you, year
after year, decade after decade: Yes, yes I will.

Awesomely beautiful! I wish I'd thought of this!

45

Young Girl at Walgreen's

Her thin legs
bruised
and knob-kneed,

she stood
in the cosmetics
aisle, her fingers

dancing over
tubes of lipstick
as if they

were piano keys,
and she, learning
a new song.

Rock 'n' Roll

Saturday morning, the sun came up like a brick
tossed through the window. Hoping to get a few
more hours of sleep, he groped around for a t-shirt
to cover his bloodshot eyes, in a pile of dirty clothes
beside the bed. He should have stopped before
that second six-pack, but at least he remembered
drinking it. Too many times in the past, he'd found
himself on the floor of some cheap

hotel room in Bogue Chitto, Mississippi or Tickfaw,
Louisiana, surrounded by liquor bottles, cigarette butts
and naked groupies whose names he never bothered
to find out—with no recollection of how they all got
there. But that was twenty years and two wives ago,
and his drums were moldering in the basement along
with a sack-full of stage outfits and big hair
products he no longer needed.

What hair he had left was gathered into a wispy ponytail
that hung between his shoulder blades like a rescue rope
for his sagging rear end. Since getting by on looks
or talent was no longer an option, he was lucky
to have a decent-paying job and was managing, so far,
to stick to it. He had to admit, however—there was nothing
better than tossing back a cold one as soon as he walked
in the door. He stayed away from the hard

stuff these days since it made him crazy and he couldn't afford the fallout. But hey, a few beers now and then never hurt anybody, although his ex-wives no doubt disagreed with that philosophy. There wasn't a soul left in his life who cared what he did, although he still commanded a certain audience in a crowded bar once he started reminiscing about the band years. Some women seem to worship musicians, even the has-beens,

and the occasional hook-up worked better for him, anyway. Drifting into a dream, he grabbed a set of imaginary sticks and started playing a Led Zeppelin tune—sweat flying, girls gazing at him like he was an answer to prayer, and best of all, nowhere near his fiftieth birthday, which he spent home alone with a case of Bud and a carton of Camels, watching cop show re-runs on cable TV until he passed out, cold.

sad —

GIRL IN A GREEN DRESS

San Francisco, 2008

A girl wearing a green dress climbs into a cable car,
wedges her slim body
between a woman clutching

a briefcase, an old man, mouth slack with sleep. Neon
lights flash garish colors across the blank screen
of her face, and one small hand

curls in her lap like a kitten. She has a story to tell,
but don't we all, though no one tells it.
We sit in silence, our lives like sheet music

nobody bothers to play—until the street car clacks
to a halt, bells clanging,
and we make our way, quickly, to the exits—

a girl in a green dress and the rest of us, our footsteps
impossible to hear, like piano keys
pressed just short of sound.

49

BILLY CISCO

Billy Cisco was a bad boy from birth.
Even his mother said so.
He clawed his way out of her body like some wild thing
and squalled for hours at a stretch,

red-faced and angry at the world.
When he was little, he kicked dogs and tore the wings

off butterflies. In school, he played mean
pranks and never did a lick of work.
He married a local girl, who left him after a two-day
honeymoon at the Motel 6 in Fayetteville,

which was, he claimed in court, the reason he commenced
a life of crime. First it was drunk and disorderly,

then petty larceny. Finally, he tried robbing
the First Citizen's Bank with a BB gun. He was wearing
a stolen chicken suit formerly owned by his ex-wife's brother,
who used to "work the curb" for a fried chicken

franchise—but all the tellers recognized those eyes of his,
slightly crossed, one blue, one brown—and that strange

humming sound he always made when he was knee-deep
in sin. These days, you can find him serving time
at the Butner Federal Correction Complex,
where even his fellow inmates

can't stand the sight of him tromping around
the exercise yard, searching for bugs
to squish between his nicotine-
stained fingers.

Awful
tale of
someone
awful ?,
why

HALLOWEEN

On a good Halloween, the sky is black as Kenyan coffee
and light flung from windows and open doors falls
in rectangular patterns, staggered like mismatched teeth.
Cats yowl and spit from the murky gloom, while witches

cackle and stir their boiling brews with bones and broom
handles. Candles flicker through Jack-o-Lantern smiles
from the steps of every porch, and the moon hides under

a cloud shaped like a hangman's hood. Monsters lurk
behind the bushes and goblins bounce on tree branches,
as bands of costumed children roam the dark streets,

their plastic buckets brimming with candy. The wispy
bodies of ghosts drift among them and the wind whips
dead leaves that skitter beside their feet like barbed

wire dragging from a boot. As the night wears on, they
weary of tricks and treats, race home where warm baths
and tucking in await them—while skeletons dance on
chimney tops, their clanking joints haunting us all to sleep.

POMPANO

Knee-deep in sea water,
Grandma casts her line.
Just beyond the spot
where the current drags
her baited hooks,
a school of pompano
breaks the surface,
their scales gleaming
like new dimes.
She walks backward
toward the shore,
her Bermuda shorts wet
and flopping around
her legs; a hot-pink cap
pulled low on her forehead.
Her brown hands, so deft
and sure, reeling in,
letting out—will catch
them, two at a time,
all afternoon. She will
wield a knife flecked
with silver and shiny
with viscera; will roll
the sweet bits of meat
in cornmeal and fry
them for our supper.

And when the night air,
salty as pork rinds, pours
through the rusted
screens of our summer
cottage, the sound
of waves makes music
for the pompano, still
running in our dreams.

doesn't quite make it at the end

Downpour

He's there every morning:
under a bridge, by the curb,

on the sidewalk. You ignore him
like a pile of old rags you keep

tripping over, vowing to toss.
But his body smells of birds caught

in drain pipes, rotting into bone,
and his mouth is a cave filled

with bats' eyes, staring. So you
flinch when his hand reaches out,

jagged nails clawing the air
as if to save himself from falling—

walk faster, shaking misery
off your clothes like drops of rain.

I like this —

GRANDMOTHER'S LAMP

In the quiet stillness of a snowy evening,
the earth is white as angel wings and the sky
purple as lilacs pressed against the window

pane. The soft glow of Grandmother's lamp,
with its yellowed shade and pattern
of porcelain roses, falls on the antique tabletop

and the picture of my mother, the ballet
dancer, posing. From the street,
it's just another lamp in a long row of lighted

windows, but to me, it is the sweet comfort
of my grandmother's face, bent earnestly
over her needlepoint, or patiently putting together

another scrapbook of memories, pasted just so
on the page. It is her quiet certainty that this, too,
shall pass, that God hears our prayers,

and that heaven is not the stuff of fairy tales
woven to quiet our fears, but as real as the lamp
she left for me, to light my way there.

APPALACHIA

[handwritten annotation: Sounds like a thesis a statement]

The old ways are dying. Ask Virgil and Dovie Crisp,
married some sixty years. They'll tell you how they
grew their own vegetables, seasoned by sweat and rain,
how good they tasted straight from the ground
or canned, either way—better than store-bought,
that winters were long and lonesome, but Lord,

the fun they had come spring when the thrum of bee
wings, the trickle of water over cold stones and birds
chattering like women hanging sheets on a stretch

of rope—brought music back to the mountains.
They'll tell you how neighbors came calling,
strumming guitars and singing songs that everybody
knew by heart, shy boys placing their hands

on a girl's waist for the first time, old folks tapping
their feet to a tune they'll never forget: how it feels
to be a man and a woman sharing one body between
them—vessels, blood and guts—and the sweet
smell of honeysuckle tempered by the tang of wild
onion, in the soft grass down by the creek.

[handwritten annotation: this is just wierd]

UNCLE JOHN'S '55 FAIRLANE

Granddaddy said to the used car
salesman, *A teenager does not
have sense enough to trade
cars*. But no, they wouldn't
take back that two-door,

hard top, pink and black
'55 Ford Fairlane—a deal
was a deal. His face flushed red

as a McIntosh apple, heating
up the telephone line while Uncle
John stood there grinning

like the proud owner of a sweet-
as-candy car. Granddaddy
slammed down the phone,

muttering a few choice words
in the process, wondering how
a boy like this dreamer here,
or any boy for that matter,
would ever make it on his own.

HALLELUJAH

He ripped out the pews, which were made of solid oak, ate his breakfast on the altar. His scrambled eggs tasted a little papery, and orange juice lingered on his tongue like wine. But light from the stained glass windows pleased him to no end. He went about his morning routine, his face changing colors depending on where he stood and if the sun was shining. Sometimes his skin was blue as the lapis robes of saints, others a rosy pink, as if he were a cherub. But the cross atop the steeple reflected his mood far more than religious sentiment. He seldom spoke to anyone—frowned at those who spoke to him. Neighbors didn't approve of what he'd done, turning the Lord's house into his own. His family hoped that parts of every prayer uttered in that holy place still drifted through the air like dust motes, would settle on his head in such plenitude that a word or two would surely seep through it. Though he found himself saying *Amen* on occasion, it was closer to a hiccup than any sign of conversion. To this day, however—many years after the man's death and the renovation of his fine house back to its original intention, bits and pieces of hymnals he once left stacked by the curb blow about the town— and more than one sinner has been saved by finding a *Hallelujah* stuck to the sole of his shoe.

BREAST CANCER SUITE

I. MORNING

She walks home from the doctor's office
down a tree-lined sidewalk, her face
dappled with light. Birds hold fast to branches,
their feet curled like the dainty

hands of old ladies clutching tea cups.
Children dash from one side of the street
to the other, and squirrels, tails
twitching, do the same. Women push

strollers or jog by her, foreheads glistening
with sweat—all going about their business
in the town where she grew up,
near the house where she has lived

for thirty years—as if nothing has changed,
as if the world has not fallen to its knees,
as if this lone woman they are passing
is ordinary.

II. NOON

The hollow-eyed creature
in the mirror, her freezer full

of casseroles and fruit pies,
her kitchen sagging beneath

the weight of good intentions—
is someone she doesn't know,

a woman with scars for breasts
and lines etched into her face

that weren't there yesterday—
or was it the day before? She

can't remember. She only
knows that time is a watered-

down soup—enough to fill her
bowl, but she is still hungry.

III. NIGHT

Skin pale as the surface of the moon,
limbs thin as matchsticks,
she lies in bed,

saying to herself, silently—
that night is a vast, dark sea roiling
and crashing above everyone,

sick or well, and that whatever happens
to her own body,
whether she lives or dies, it will go

on doing that very thing—leaving stars
behind like shells on a beach—taking
them back, by morning.

Woman in Delhi

A young woman crosses a busy
street, holding a red umbrella.
She walks between cars stuck
in traffic, horns honking, radios

blaring—past rickshaw wallas
and meandering cattle, a man
carrying a cage of green parrots.

Regal as a queen, she moves as if
the road is strewn with flowers,
as if the world is holding its breath
until she reaches the other side.

DARLA'S DAUGHTER ✓

Darla's daughter slit her wrists again.
She watches blood bead and trickle
from the thin lines her brother's pen knife
makes. Her brother is a good boy, an Eagle
Scout and *never a bit of trouble*, her mother
always says. But man is she a mess, Darla's
daughter, and no one speaks of her without
sighing. So she sits on the edge of the tub,
not really serious about dying—or living,
either, for that matter. She'd prefer to drift
between the two like a baby seahorse with
its tiny perfect body that looks exactly like
all the other baby seahorse bodies. She
is tired of wearing the heavy mantle of her
own unique perfection—the porcelain skin
and towering height that prompt awestruck
strangers to stop her in the street, ask if she's
a model. Weightless, floating—*that's what
I want*, she thinks as her mother bursts through
the door screaming, wraps her daughter's
wrists in towels and rushes her to the hospital.
The doctor says her life was *never in danger*,
the cuts were *shallow*, and Darla's daughter
laughs. She knows how eagerly her heart opened
its chambered mouth and sucked the knife in.

Good —

Awesome last line.

63

IV

SHRIMP BOAT CAPTAIN

The craggy-faced shrimp boat captain
keeps a pinch of chewing tobacco between
his lip and gum, wears faded blue overalls
and a ball cap. Early mornings, you'll
find him lumbering down the road towards
an old wooden pier, carrying a cooler filled
with ice, a fishing rod slung over his beefy
shoulder. Tackle swings like a pendulum
behind his back until he reaches his favorite
bench, close to the end. He pulls a bag
of shrimp from the cooler, baits his hooks
and casts his line as far as arthritis allows—
sits there until noon, either catching fish
or not; it's all the same to him. It's the sun
and wind and rain he's come for—the view
of shrimp boats headed out to sea, crews
tiny as toy soldiers. He can hear the cries
of hungry gulls, feel each vessel's pitch
and toss, though he is captain of nothing
now, save his own soul. And what his soul
wants is to keep his body close to water—
until the moon captures him in her net and lifts
it with cool, white hands into the starry sky.

CRYSTAL CLEAR

She's the girl sitting in a row of fake leather seats beside
a bald man unwrapping a pastrami sandwich
and a baby staring

at her glassy-eyed, from his dinged-up stroller. Her eyelashes
are stuck together in kohl-colored clumps, and she's
fingering a loop of plastic

beads she stole yesterday from the K-Mart. She's thinking
nobody ever loved her as far
as she can tell—

not even her own mother, who sells herself for drugs and hard
liquor down by the railroad tracks,
who said Crystal's daddy

was *everyman.* After spending the night alone again in their
singlewide trailer while neighbor boys pawed
the flimsy front door,

she took the tin filled with cash her mother kept buried
in the back yard and bought a bus ticket
to Wilmington. She heard they make movies

there just like they do in Hollywood. With her silky
blonde hair and near-perfect features, she believes she has what
it takes to become

a famous movie star or even a movie star's girlfriend,
which might be even better. When her bus pulls into the station,
she climbs up the stairs

and settles herself beside a drab looking middle-aged woman
with bruised knees and cracked, red hands,
who's probably been scrubbing

floors her whole life. Crystal would rather eat glass than
crawl around in other people's houses
for a living.

The one thing she learned from her mother was never sell
your body for less than what it's worth or at least
something you can't do without,

which wasn't much as far as Crystal was concerned, since
she'd spent the past sixteen years surviving
with nothing at all.

I don't like — cliched stereotypes

BOOGIE-WOOGIE

Nobody taught our father to play,
but he could crank out a boogie-woogie
beat on his sister's piano,

fingers bouncing on the keys like ten
happy children, feet tapping—
smiling

like he never did before he left for work
or came home, tired. He'd collapse
on the couch,

loosen his belt—become so still
in sleep, you'd think
he wasn't breathing. But Dad could fly

across a keyboard—his body so light,
we put our hands on his shoulders
to keep him on the ground.

Ties That Bind ✓

Muriel bustles around her mother's room at the nursing home, trying to please her. She already bought four pastel housecoats with front pockets because *Mama* won't wear any other kind. She spent the night before washing her mother's underwear and terrycloth slippers, rolling thin, white socks into matching pairs before moving on to balancing the checkbook and paying medical bills from her dwindling account. Today is shampoo day, so she'll wheel *Mama* to the beauty shop where she screams when they touch her, as if she's being murdered. She is jealous, too, if her daughter speaks to other residents. Muriel ignores the daggered looks her mother throws when she leans down to hug the old women whose children never visit. She refuses to curb her kindness for approval she will never get, anyway. But Muriel continues to care for her mother without complaint—a woman who grows more petulant with every passing year. As *Mama* sinks ever deeper into a chair padded with just the right number and thickness of pillows, (her bones turning into Styrofoam), Muriel will get clumsier. She will drop brushes and combs, bobby pins and nail files because carrying disapproval is like bringing a full load of laundry up the stairs with no basket. Something always slips from your grasp. But she will enter that room with a smile on her face, as if it's the only place she wants to be in the whole world, including Rio de Janeiro and Paris. She will plump pillows and dispense hugs like Pez until the very last breath her mother takes, which will be a relief to almost everyone concerned, particularly Mama, who will rush toward heaven like a mouse from whose back a piano has been lifted, while Muriel mourns and feels guilty, convinced she could have done more.

Not a poem —

At the Pediatrician's Office

In 1961, Dr. Street was so old his first name
could have been Adam. His stethoscope dangled
like an elephant's trunk against
his wrinkled dress shirt,

sleeves rolled to the elbows as if we
were a dirty job, but somebody had to do it.

His nurse was taller than a water tower,
her smile teeming with baby toes, caught between
her teeth at breakfast. She enjoyed

injections, you could tell—plunging the needle in,
leaving a bruise behind like a signature.

Terrified, but too proud to whimper
when our names were called, we'd march solemn-faced
across the waiting room—miniature Marie
Antoinettes, making our way to the guillotine.

SPRINGTIME IN BEAUFORT

A tangle of tourists wearing dark sunglasses
and baggy shorts stands on a dock by the channel,

eating blueberry muffins left over from complimentary
hotel breakfasts, and talking

among themselves, their voices a comforting murmur
to a half-dozen babies dozing in strollers. A boat

named *Angel Ray* bobs in the water, seagulls circling
a mast so tall, a lone cloud lifts her white skirt

higher as she drifts past, to keep from snagging the hem.
Shopkeepers jangling giant sets of keys bustle down

the sidewalks toward their gift stores and ice cream
shops, hoping the scant, pre-season crowd will follow.

But people aren't yet thinking of goods they wish
to buy. For now, the salt-scented breeze

and the sound of seawater splashing against the boards
is enough to keep them content—while spring

rolls slowly into Beaufort like a parade of beauty queens
in rose-covered floats, gloved hands waving.

Making the Biscuits

Wearing a plain cotton dress and work boots,
gray braids pinned to her head, my great-grandmother
bent down, scooped a palm-full of flour from a sack
on the floor, tossed it on the wooden block
beneath the window. Her hands, thick-knuckled,
arthritic—mixed, kneaded

and rolled wet dough as she stood in the narrow
pantry—a wall of shelves weighted with canned
vegetables on one side, dish towels drying
from a rope near the other. Flour rose

like puffs of smoke from her hands, floated
around her body in such profusion, it must have
seemed that she was fading from this world,
or had only just materialized from another.

By all accounts, she was a hard woman,
but Granny's biscuits were light as clouds—
soft in the center, crusty on top, perfect
for sopping up redeye gravy or Blackstrap

molasses. But first, she had to make them, day
after day, week after week, year after year—
before the sun rose over the distant trees, its face
round as the biscuit cutter she jabbed again
and again on the flour-dusted dough, her motions
quick as an adder, striking.

AFTER THE DIAGNOSIS

Naked, she poses in front of a full-length
mirror, morning light pouring through
the window like bleach. She's gazing at her
body as if she is a lover, seeing it for the last
time—her long neck, the fine blonde hairs
on her legs and arms—her breasts, which
doctors want to remove before the cancer
kills her. They seem so innocent—girlish
aureoles pink as a nursery, one side a little
larger than the other, but not much. She
remembers the first boy who ever kissed her
there, how warm his breath felt, blowing
across her skin—wonders what she will feel
when her breasts are gone. She was happy
once, without them—climbing trees, riding
a bicycle, playing tag with her friends—
but can't imagine, somehow, a flat chest on
her middle-aged body. Yet, it will happen,
and soon. *Let them take my breasts to save
my life*, she thinks, but she will keep the kiss.

*Really?
Seems so
unlikely
this would be
the reaction*

THE GARDENER

The gardener walks five miles
to work, most of it uphill. He doesn't
mind. Each morning he stops to pray
for his wife and sons at St. Leo's
Church, halfway to the grounds
of his employer's grand estate—
and the tiny shed where he keeps
his tools, immaculate.

From her bedroom window,
the boss's daughter watches him
work. She is wealthy beyond

imagination, but it seems to him,
unhappy. *It is not my business,*
he tells himself, and there is much

to do every day, in her father's
garden. The daughter loves
the gardener from afar, not because

he is young or handsome, which he
is not. It is his gentleness with plants,
the way he tends to them like newborns,
how he talks to them, no matter
who is listening. She longs, in fact,
to be the gardener's daughter,
to feel the breath of his affection.
Then she, too, might bloom.

INCIDENT ON THE TRAIN

Wearing gold lamé shorts
and a halter top,
she boarded the train at Harlem.
Her nails were ten red

hooks curling toward
her palms, her blonde wig
askew. Convinced he stole
her cigarettes,

she argued with a white
man, four rows up, who refused
to hand them over,
claiming he didn't smoke

and "by the way,"
he said, "you're crazy." She
replied, "at least I ain't
no thief."

ROBERT'S RECOLLECTION OF HEATING 21 NASSAU

Covered in dials, valves and pipes, the old furnace
was a miracle of cast iron engineering, requiring a regular
supply of *Blue Coal*, proud sponsor of *The Shadow*,*
said Robert, leaning back in his chair, smiling.

The bed of the Osborne & Marsellas coal truck would lift
skyward, *hydraulics groaning*, and bricks of coal
would tumble into wire and canvas buckets.
Then the coal carriers hoisted

the brimming buckets onto their burly shoulders, *schlepped
them up eleven stairs* to the house and dumped them into
a slide that carried the coal to a bin. *It was a filthy
business*, he said, *but the hiss*

of steam rising from the radiator vents created a *cozy heat*
on cold winter mornings in New England, warming
every room at 21 Nassau, the recollection
of which, warms him still.

*The Shadow *is a collection of serialized dramas on 1930's radio.*

Homecoming

In memory of Edwin Linville

> "And God shall wipe away all tears
> from their eyes; and there shall be no
> more death, neither sorrow, nor crying,
> neither shall there be any more pain…"
> *Revelation 21:4*

Suddenly, Edwin felt lighter,
like a boy stepping out of heavy
winter shoes to dart across a field,
though he wasn't in a field at all.
He was standing on a railroad track,
rails still warm from a passing train.
He could hear it in the distance—
wheels clacking, whistle blowing long
and lonesome, though he wasn't alone.
There was a man walking towards
him, slow and steady, as if he had
a thousand years to get where he
was going. Something about him
looked familiar—the planes of his face,
the slope of his shoulders—his clothes
old-fashioned and spotlessly clean.
Then he smiled and Edwin knew
who it was, instantly. Younger than
he'd ever seen him, it was *Papa*—
his beloved grandfather, long gone
but never once, forgotten. Edwin
wanted to meet him halfway, but he
was an old man who could barely

cross a room these days without
collapsing. Yet his legs felt strong
enough to carry him around the world
and back, and his hands were smooth
and suntanned, veins fat with blood
that seemed to surge through them,
swift as water in a stream. And *Papa*—
he was laughing now—kneeling down,
arms outstretched. So Edwin started
running, years falling from his body
like autumn leaves—until he was
a child again, so glad to be home.

making a lot of assumptions here —

SANDPIPER

Searching
for breakfast along
the ocean's edge,

a sandpiper,
with specks
of foam quivering

on its beak, darts
to and fro across
the wet sand,

its feet smaller
than a fingernail,
then skitters

down the beach—
alone, save for
its shadow.

LUNCH TIME

When I opened my Barbie lunchbox,
the essence of other lunches lingered alongside
the carefully wrapped ham and cheese

sandwich, the slightly soft apple. Pickle
juice that leaked into corners and crevasses,
left a trail of brine. Peanut butter wiped

away, still offered up its nutty essence,
it's long-term relationship with grape jelly.
But what I remember best is the cherry

and almond scent of my mother's hands—
how it clung to the wax paper, the neatly folded
napkin—how she left traces of herself

behind, like snails drawing circles on a sidewalk:
loops of lustrous pearl that shimmer like love
would, if we could see it shining.

very nice

I really like the sentiment of this poem more that the exact words

83

V

WAYFARER

He seems like a man
you'd see walking down a long
stretch of road, the kind
with dust

rising

in a red haze beneath the wheels
of pickup trucks, cutting
through fields of golden

wheat. Scudding clouds cast
shadows
across the ground like whales

mixed metaphor

swimming through clear
water, and the air carries the scent
of grain and loam.

Every few miles, the glint of a silo
(startling against the lonesome

sky)

signals a farm house
where peach pies sit cooling

on window sills, and patterned
carpets are worn-out from parents

pacing to and fro with fretful babies
in their arms.

He's traveling toward the horizon
with the steady gait of someone
with a place to go, whose tender

gaze

will soon find home, that place
more sacred than communion wafers
nestled in the palms
of angels.

where she gets the title

INTERLUDE ✓ *Nurse*

Last night I dreamed a kiss, your mouth
empty of every word your lips
had been saying. There were arias
in the silence of your breath,

like the sighs of young lovers reaching
for the same slice of bread.

It is in caesurae that I love you best,
in spaces hallowed and quiet
as cathedrals, where nothing is spoken,
but every thing is said.

LOUISE HICKMAN

Steeped in a vat of sin is what I am, thought Brother Bob
Braithwaite, on his knees again—probably for some minor
offense like jaywalking or saying *gosh darn*,
his administrative assistant, Louise Hickman, said to herself.
She sat right outside his office door and could hear him
in there, pleading for forgiveness.

Louise was nowhere near as nice as she pretended
to be. She was downright ornery,
if truth be known, and a closet atheist. The few close

friends who knew about her anti-religion sentiments
wondered why on earth she worked at the Baptist church.
Louise just told them it was convenient

to her house, but the real reason was her passion for Brother Bob
His very presence made her mouth go dry and her heart thump
and carry on until she thought she'd have to call 911

when he walked into a room. She hated to spend even one
day without him. Why, come weekends,
she nearly pined herself to death until Monday mornings

when she drove back to work singing the Hallelujah Chorus
in falsetto. Fortunately, Brother Bob
was a single man—but his commitment to the Lord

was so overwhelming and absolute, there was no room
in his life for romance. But you better believe
if he ever changed his mind,
Louise Hickman would be waiting for him with a pair
of everlasting arms—you can count on that.

This is not poetry. Flash maybe, but much, much too prosy

BACK PORCH BLUES

She sat on the back porch sucking
on a cigarette, listening to a Muddy Waters
CD, when her recent ex-husband pulled
up in his Chevy Malibu, parked and cut the engine.
He gripped the steering wheel

like a sea captain keeping a ship on course,
while his car leaked oil on her clean driveway.
She took one last drag, flipped
the smoldering butt in the wet grass
and went inside, locking the screen behind

her. She felt guilty about her lack of hospitality,
but every conversation with her ex-husband
turned into an argument and she was in a mellow
mood. So she stood on her tiptoes, leaned
over the couch they bought together

at a yard sale, and peeked through the mini blinds.
By then, he'd rolled down the window
and his fingers were tapping on the car door,
keeping time to her music. She considered calling
the police since you never could tell what

people were going to do, particularly when
they came out on the short end of a divorce
settlement. But before she could make up her mind,
he cranked the motor and drove away. She
wondered why he came by in the first place,

but maybe he caught himself doing what she
did sometimes—cruising down the highway,
radio blaring, feeling good until she reached across
the seat for someone who wasn't there—
and pulled her hand back, empty.

Not a poem for me
Flashin stanzas

Riding Gun's Bicycle to Lake Mälaren

Västerås, Sweden

Gun's bicycle was wobbly and dinged,
its fenders rusty and tires close to flat,
but its worn whicker basket was full of happy
memories, and it still made the trip
from the cottage to the lake.

Pausing near the water's edge,
I watched the soft light of day harden
into gold. Spangled trees rimmed
the shoreline, and boats bobbed in their slips

like rows of old men, nodding
off to sleep. Then I pedaled back the way
I came—up the road and through the garden,
where Gun stood on the dusk-laden path,
her face like a lantern, glowing.

I just don't like her style, her voice

SAM WHITE

Sam White in bib overalls and a pork pie hat
set off down the road, slow-paced and drowsy-eyed.
It was early Monday morning, June, mist swirling
around tree trunks and hanging over creek water
like nature-loving ghosts. His wife told him the day
before to fetch a watermelon from the old man
with the raspy voice who sold them from his truck.
Sam was looking forward to jawing with the vendor
for a spell, but the man's son was there, instead—
a sallow-faced, sickly looking boy who hawked up
more phlegm than his daddy. So Sam thumped a few
melons, hoisted the best one on his broad shoulder,
and dropped some coins into the boy's outstretched
hand. He took the long way home, crossed a meadow
filled with flowers, the names he didn't know *but they
sure are pretty* is what he was thinking—unaware
that his own eyes were the same color blue. Sam
White never was one to gaze into mirrors or much care
what he looked like as long as he was clean. He kept
walking until he came to his daughter's backyard
where he kneeled down and stowed that melon under
a bush to keep cool until evening, when his son-in-law
would carve it into rounds and salt the juicy meat
for the grandchildren, whose eager grins were what Sam
White lived for now that his working days were done.

95

Mizuko Jizo

On the days she makes amends,
a mother kneels beside her *Mizuko Jizo*.
There are thousands like it in the temple
at Kamakura, effigies of lost
children—miscarried, stillborn, aborted—
and parents who come there to care

for them. She pours water over the statue
to quench her child's thirst, ties
a sweater around its shoulders to warm
the stone. It takes many hours
to knit these garments when the needles
tremble in your hands,

and your heart feels like a skein of yarn,
unraveling. She prays for safe passage
for the baby's spirit, speaks a name that only
she among the living knows.
Then she rises like a wisp of smoke—
walks away alone.

Sad story poorly told —

SUNFLOWERS

In our well-manicured yard
where a clover can't show its face
or risk dire consequences, a row
of sunflowers sprang up by the bird
feeder, claiming the kitchen

window for their own. Such thick
stalks and heavy flowers belong
in children's stories, where
gardens bloom in shapes
and colors seldom imagined

and mushrooms grow as big
as houses. With great dark eyes
surrounded by yellow lashes,
they follow the sun on its daily
journey—a bevy of bold young

girls in love with the same boy.
Dazzling beauties all, showing
up our prim blades of grass
and trimmed bushes like hula
dancers in a room full of pilgrims.

An Old Woman Looks Out the Window on Christmas Morning

Her husband calls it snow, a word
she doesn't remember but it feels
good in her mouth, that word—
creamy, in fact, with bits of bark

and earth crumbled into it, and holly
berries. And it is cold, so cold—
she can feel it through the glass.

Yet her husband's breath is warm
and he is smiling, as if there are

no glowering clouds and the road
is not impassable beneath this glaring

whiteness. "The grandchildren
will be here soon," he says, whoever
they are. And then she forgets

everything he said because this
moment is all she has and the next

moment comes with no memory
of the one before—so she asks
again and again, "What is it?" until

at last he tells her, "It's Christmas,
Darling, Christmas," and takes
her into his arms, where she doesn't
care, anymore, about words.

Lovely!

Roy Rogers Rides Again

Walking down the stairs into the old Sears
building downtown, you could smell fresh
buttered popcorn as soon as the glass doors
opened, and feel the occasional crushed kernel
under your Keds as you went along—past
the assorted loose candies and sales girls
waiting to scoop it up and bag it for you.
Candy corn was my favorite, with its garish
colors and the taste of pure cane sugar dissolving
in your mouth. But the best thing in the store,
even better than the toy department with its
cap guns and baby dolls, was the mechanical
pony with his shiny brown coat, black tail
and mane—all four of his legs stretched straight
out like he was blazing across the prairie,
his painted eyes wild with joy. He had a saddle
with real leather stirrups, and reins you could
hold in your hands. And if your dad parted
with the spare change in his pockets or your
mom found a few coins in the bottom of her
purse, you could jump on the pony's back
long enough to capture the bad guys, save
the town, and ride off into the sunset.

BUDDY

Buddy, wearing his butterscotch
smoking jacket with the cream-colored

accents, lounged around the house
flexing his toes in multiple
stretches, his yawns so lengthy and wide,

you could count his teeth twice.
He was never in a hurry—slinked
rather than walked, unless something

of interest crossed his path, in which case,
he loped. He loved our daughter

to distraction, would let her drape his body
around her shoulders like a cat stole—
but would claw anyone else who dared

to pick him up. He had his dignity
to consider, after all, though he abandoned

it happily, for her. He slept through most
nights, but at the first crack of dawn, would

leap on our feet as if they were chipmunks
hiding under the bed covers—a hint
that he was hungry.

Buddy knew somehow, when one of us
was sad—would sit close beside the gloomy
party, purring madly,

as if to remind us that we still had friends.
We like to imagine, now that he's gone,
Buddy lolling around heaven,

taking frequent naps, but making sure
that all the angels get up early.

Another
cat person

The Onion Eater

The Onion Eater peels another layer of onion—
slips a piece into her mouth, the edge of a blade
flashing in the noon-day sun. Most people pass
by with hardly a glance—accustomed to seeing
her sitting in that ladder-back chair outside the post
office, a bucket of onions on the ground beside her.
Once a towheaded boy around six years old stopped
and said, "Lady, how come you eat onions all day
long?" The Onion Eater turned her head slowly,
watched him while she chewed and swallowed—
tears streaming down the wrinkles in her cheeks,
wetting the front of her dress in patches. The boy
backed away from the fierceness of her gaze,
which seemed to fasten on him like a steam shovel
lifting dirt. "Could be, I like the taste of onions,"
she said, leaning in close. "I bet you cry on a dime,
don't you, boy?" Too scared to lie, he nodded.
"Next time, thank the Lord Jesus for them tears.
Some people can't cry—even when the pain's
so bad, they is on their knees. If I didn't eat onions,"
she said, pulling a choice Vidalia from the bucket,
"I'd drown in misery that won't come out." She
looked past him then, as if he wasn't there, as if she
saw something so terrible, he couldn't even imagine
it. So the boy took off running, sending onion skins
flying around her legs and feet like translucent birds.

FARMERS' MARKET

The scent of peaches rose from his hands
as he stood behind the counter,
weighing fruit. Slashed across both cheeks

were twin tattoos—marks that could have
been made by ink-stained claws.
What do they mean?

the customer asked, staring. He counted
out change, pooled pennies
in her upturned palm. *Once I worked*

for a corporation, he said, then pointed
to his face—*these make sure I can never
go back.* He watched her walk

away, his eyes clear as well water, his old
life shifting on the bottom
like a wooden bucket, rotting.

LOVE

A middle-aged couple watches the sun
set from their own back porch. Birds
sing, the sound sweet in the muggy air
of a summer evening—yet sweeter still,
the soft murmur of their voices, chatting
about nothing more important than what
they had for lunch, how nice the weather
has been of late. Perhaps even God slows
down His fevered pace of prayer-answering
and soul-saving, to listen to them speak,
to watch them lean toward one another
like two trees long rooted on the same hill.
Perhaps it feels to Him like nights when we,
as children, fall asleep in the backseat of
the family car, our parents' idle conversation
like a lullaby, singing *you are safe, you are
loved*—and God sighs, just to think of it.

WAVES

For Tommy, 1959-1980

Standing waist-deep in the ocean, arms stiff
at our sides like soldiers at attention, we could hear
the waves winding like cartoon fists behind our backs,
feel the suck and pull of water on our sunburned
skins. According to the rules, we couldn't turn
around. If you did, you were *chicken*. We cheated
sometimes, if the roar was too loud, the tide too
strong—but mostly, every wave surprised

us. Some were gentle swells that left us standing;
others pushed our bodies sideways, but didn't sweep
us off our feet. And then there were the rogue
waves that curled above our heads—palms full
of broken shells and seaweed, small fish
sticking to their fingers

like glitter. One slap and we were tumbling
through the murky, sand-swirled sea, elbows scraping
the rough bottom until we washed up on shore—
battered, bruised and often bleeding. It's harder now,
the knock down and tumble of life, the getting up
again, but I do it—remembering how you
always laughed, rose from your knees
and hit the waves, running.

Tender
Interesting

AT THE DRIVE-IN

You parked your father's car in this very field
and hurried to the concession stand, dodging lightning
bugs and wayward children running from their mothers.

As you stood in line, you glanced over your shoulder
at the yellow-haired girl whose hands rested in her lap

like fresh-picked lilies, who smiled at you like you were
someone she'd been waiting for all her life; except you
didn't think such things back then. You only knew that she

was with you voluntarily, which seemed to you a miracle—
and if you managed not to spill your drink on her dress
or snag her lip with your braces, she might let you touch

some small part of her skin, however briefly. So you
slid in beside her, fixed the speaker to the window. You
watched the actors move and speak and play out their

scripted lives on the whitewashed shingles of a makeshift
movie screen, but what you remember most are the stars

that twinkled all around it, and how her hair felt soft
as leaves brushing against your cheek. And even now,
years later, the concession stand closed, the ticket booth

locked—the screen fallen to its wooden knees in the tall
grass—the stars still twinkle above the abandoned
field, and the old man gazing up at them, smiling.

Personal Acknowledgments

As ever, I'm grateful to God for every precious day, for all the blessings in my life including my wonderful family and friends. Thanks, also, for giving me a sense of humor. It comes in handy.

My love and eternal gratitude to my husband, Leonard, my parents, Tom and Loretta Kirby, my daughter and son-in-law, Gia and Matt, and my uncle, artist Stephen White, whose stunning paintings have graced the covers of all my books.

Special thanks to our dear family friend, Frances Y. Dunn, to whom the cover painting for *In the Palms of Angels*, entitled, "Frances," is lovingly dedicated.

To Susan Nagel-Bloch, Fran Kiger, Pamela Byrd, Maricam Kaleel, Debra Hardiman, Mick Scott, Joan Nichols, Debbie Kincaid, Harriet Strickland, Phil Montemayor, Art Nadelman, Stella Gibson, Tim Plowman, Charity Smosna, Mark C. Houston, Gene and Mary Bond, Rita Phillips, the "Susans" (Collie and Smith), Yong Tang, and John Beck—thank you for being there for me. I don't know what I'd do without your friendship and support.

Thanks, also, to writers/friends Sharon Randall, Ron Powers, Kathryn Stripling Byer, Guy Neal Williams, Felicia Mitchell, Frank Elliott, Sara Claytor, Crystal Sage, Richard Krawiec, Frank Sundram, Helen Losse, Meg Pokrass and a long list of others, too numerous to name. I appreciate you more than I can say.

I'd like to recognize the following people who are no longer "with us," for inspiring poems in this collection: Sam and Nannie White, John Henry and Blanche Kirby, Ila White, Edwin Linville, Angeline Myers, Robert M. Kerr, Gun Ericsson, Ursula Beck, Rose Rusch, and my beloved "little" brother, Thomas "Tommy" M. Kirby, Jr.

Additionally, I'd like to express my thanks to Chaplain Joanne Henley of the Derrick L. Davis Forsyth Regional Cancer Center, for her compassionate care of so many, and for believing in the healing power of poetry and art.

To Elizabeth Reynolds, my fifth grade teacher at Brunson Elementary School, for her gifted teaching that has remained with me throughout my life, and for introducing me to poetry. (Note to Mrs. Reynolds: Remember when my best buddy Vickie Johnson and I carved William Wordsworth's head out of a bar of soap?)

To Jim and Cathy Tedder, owners of the Community Arts Café in Winston-Salem, NC—I so appreciate their dedication to and support of writers and artists. And thanks to the owners and employees of every bookstore, specialty shop, art gallery, etc., where books of poetry are sold, and to poetry readers, bless you.

To my friend and publisher, Kevin Morgan Watson, words are not enough to thank you.

As far as I'm concerned, you are all angels.

Photo by Superieur Photographics

TERRI KIRBY ERICKSON is the award-winning author of two previous collections of poetry, including *Telling Tales of Dusk*, which was published by Press 53 in 2009 and reached #23 on The Poetry Foundation Contemporary Best Sellers list in 2010. Her poetry has appeared in numerous literary journals, anthologies and publications, including *The Christian Science Monitor*, *JAMA* and the *North Carolina Literary Review*, and has been nominated for the Pushcart Prize and Best of the Net Award. Her awards include First Prize honors from the North Carolina Poetry Society, The Writers' Ink Guild and the Carteret Writers Award for Poetry. She lives in a small town in North Carolina with her husband, Leonard—where most of the time it's so quiet you can hear a cloud's wheels squeak as it rolls across the sky.

About the Cover Artist

STEPHEN WHITE specializes in figurative paintings done on wood in gold leaf and transparent oil glazes. His work is available through the Little Art Gallery in Raleigh, North Carolina, and Village Smith Gallery in Winston-Salem, North Carolina.

CPSIA information can be obtained
at www.ICGtesting.com
Printed in the USA
BVHW07s1742200618
519235BV00003B/43/P